Philip Slaughter

**A Sketch of the Life of Randolph Fairfax**

A Private in the Ranks of the Rockbridge Artillery, Attached to the...

Philip Slaughter

**A Sketch of the Life of Randolph Fairfax**
*A Private in the Ranks of the Rockbridge Artillery, Attached to the...*

ISBN/EAN: 9783337021405

Printed in Europe, USA, Canada, Australia, Japan

Cover: Foto ©ninafisch / pixelio.de

More available books at **www.hansebooks.com**

# A SKETCH

OF

# THE LIFE

OF

# RANDOLPH FAIRFAX,

A PRIVATE IN THE RANKS OF THE ROCKBRIDGE ARTILLERY, ATTACHED TO
THE "STONEWALL BRIGADE" AND SUBSEQUENTLY TO THE 1st
REGT. VA. LIGHT ARTILLERY, 2D CORPS ARMY OF
NORTHERN VIRGINIA; INCLUDING A
BRIEF ACCOUNT OF

## JACKSON'S CELEBRATED VALLEY CAMPAIGN.

BY THE

## REV. PHILIP SLAUGHTER,

*Editor of the "Army and Navy Messenger"*

~~~~~~~~

RICHMOND, VA.
TYLER, ALLEGRE & McDANIEL, ENQUIRER JOB OFFICE
1864.

SECOND EDITION.

# A SKETCH

## THE LIFE

OF

# RANDOLPH FAIRFAX,

A PRIVATE IN THE RANKS OF THE ROCKBRIDGE ARTILLERY, ATTACHED TO
THE "STONEWALL BRIGADE" AND SUBSEQUENTLY TO THE 1ST
REGT. VA. LIGHT ARTILLERY, 2D CORPS, ARMY OF
NORTHERN VIRGINIA: INCLUDING A
BRIEF ACCOUNT OF

## JACKSON'S CELEBRATED VALLEY CAMPAIGN.

BY THE

# REV. PHILIP SLAUGHTER,

*Editor of the "Army and Navy Messenger."*

~~~~~~

RICHMOND, VA.
TYLER, ALLEGRE & McDANIEL, ENQUIRER JOB OFFICE.
1864.

# INTRODUCTION.

---

Gray's Elegy in a country churchyard, owes its world-wide popularity, not merely to the elegance of the language and the musical flow of the verses, but chiefly to the fact that it is a true expression of the thoughts and feelings which such a scene naturally awakens in the human mind. Few could have painted the picture, but every enlightened person recognizes in it his own likeness. If such a subject as a single country churchyard inspired such a poem in an ungenial clime, what a grand elegy the Poet would have written had he been born in our day in the sunny South, whose soil is cut up with sepulchres, and whose blue sky is the ceiling of a vast series of vaults in which are entombed hosts of young cavaliers, who had they been developed by time and culture, might have commanded the applause of listening Senators or swayed the rod of empire. When old men die it seems almost as natural, and awakens but little more emotion than when the evening sun goes down. When little infants in their early dawn close their soft eyes and breathe no more, we wonder what could have been the design of an All-wise Providence in bringing into the world so many young immortals just to look around them and to die. But when the maid in the bud of her beauty and the young man in the bloom of his youth, standing in the midst of the landscape, and while hope is gladdening their vision with its enchanting perspectives, are suddenly cut down like the flower, " these are the tombs that claim the tender tear and the elegiac song." But men in the ranks generally have no poet, and they die not unwept but "unhonored and unsung."

Officers reap all the honors of war. While they live their brows are crowned with laurels, and their ears are regaled with the sweet music of praise. And when they die, their names and memories go down to future ages embodied in monumental marble or emblazoned upon the pictured pages of History. " Officers therefore may have motives other than the cause. But the soldier in the ranks can have none. He knows that his valor must generally pass unnoticed save in the narrow circle of his company; that his sacrifices can bring no honor to himself nor reputation to his family." He knows that if he survives, he lives only to enter upon new dangers, with the same hopelessness of distinction; that if he dies he will fall unepitaphed, perhaps uncoffined; and yet he goes into battle with unfaltering steps, proud to do his duty. His comrades fall around him thick and fast, yet with a sigh and tear, he closes his ranks and presses on to a like destiny. Sublime devotion! If honor should be given "to whom honor is due," then let us render everlasting honor to " the noble army of martyrs" whose blood cries to Heaven from the ground on which they fell, and to those who yet fill the ranks of the Confederate Army.

# CHAPTER I.

*Randolph's ancestry—His personal appearance—His dutifulness—
The boat incident—His excursion through the North—His acquaintance with Mr. Dewy.*

The subject of this sketch was a private in the
ranks. The blood of two historical families met in
his veins, and are both represented in his name—
Randolph Fairfax. Randolph was the son of Dr.
Orlando Fairfax, of Alexandria, who is the grand-
son of Rev. Bryan Fairfax, who was the Rector of
Fairfax parish, in the county of Fairfax, and who
inherited the title of Lord Fairfax. His mother
was the daughter of Jefferson Cary and Virginia
Randolph, the sister of Governor Thomas Mann
Randolph, who married the daughter of Thomas
Jefferson, the author of the Declaration of Ameri-
can Independence, and the Father of the University
of Virginia. Randolph was born in the city of
Alexandria, Va., on the 23d of November, 1842.
From his infancy he was remarkable for an almost
womanly beauty. His eyes were hazel and his hair
of a golden brown, his features regular and his
complexion brilliant. These soft beauties, as he
grew in stature, were developed into a manly form,
which, though not tall, was distinguished for a noble
and graceful bearing. His outward form was the
fair index of inward purity. Even in his childhood,
there was an absence of the waywardness and fits
of passion which generally characterise that age.
From his earliest years it was said of him by those
who knew him best, " Randolph is actuated by a
desire to do his duty; his conduct seems to be gov-
erned by principle." After passing through an in-
fant school with great credit, he entered at ten years

of age, the High School of Alexandria, kept by that
excellent Preceptor Benjamin Hallowell. Even
then there was so much blended dignity and gentleness in his bearing that his teacher was wont to
say of him, "Randolph is a little gentleman," and
his associates never treated him with rudeness nor
took those liberties, to repel which demands the
exhibition of what is called spirit in a boy. He
was much beloved by his school fellows, because,
they said Randolph never got angry and always
played fairly. And yet he was not grave nor austere.
None partook with more glee than he of the games
of the playground, or displayed more agility and
skill in them. The following incident will illus-
trate his sense of duty, even at that early age. He
was a member of a boating club which used on summer afternoons to go rowing on the Potomac river.
Sailing had been prohibited by his mother as dan-
gerous. At dinner one day, he said to his mother,
"The boys of our club want to have a sail this
afternoon, may I join them"? She replied, " No,
my son, the day is very hot and I am sure there will
be a storm, and I should not have a moments peace
if I knew you were on the river in a sail-boat!" He
said no more, but late in the evening he came in
heated and dusty and told his mother that the boys
when they found he could not join them in a sail,
gave it up, "and we rowed, he said, four miles up the
river. The wind was then fair for sailing and they
wished to raise the sail. I insisted upon their
doing it and made them put me ashore and I walked
home. " It was hard to do, mamma", he said, " and
I have had a very hot walk, but I could not disobey
you." The example had its effect upon his young
companions, for the mother of one of them remarked in a few days to Randolph's father, "you may
trust that boy anywhere."

In the months of August and September, 1854, Randolph made a visit to his aunt, Mrs. Gouverneur Morris of New York, who had a son near his own age, and accompanied them on a tour throughout the Northern States. During this tour he visited many places famous as the scenes of interesting events in our first Revolution. His uncle, Mr. Morris, being well acquainted with these places and their historical associations, made the excursion both delightful and profitable to him. While on a steamboat on Lake Champlain, a gentleman attracted by his looks, walked up to Randolph and entered into conversation with him, asking his name, and introducing himself as Mr. Dewy, of New York, once a Senator of that State. On learning Randolph's name, he remarked. "I would not like to have a name already so famous that I could add nothing to it." Randolph replied, "It is the name of my ancestors, and if they have made it famous, I at least will try to do nothing to impair its brightness." This gentleman continued with the party, and was several days with Randolph at Saratoga, and when they parted solicited a correspondence with him. Mr. Dewy was a man between thirty and forty years of age and of considerable literary attainments. He frequently sent Randolph copies of his speeches and lectures. For some years he also had books and other new publications sent by the publishers in New York to Randolph at his several schools. His letters, which we have had the pleasure of reading, were quite romantic in their expression of friendship, and modestly apologised for intruding on one who already had so many to love him.

tracing the ideal type of a perfect woman, gives her a grandmother for her instructress, remarking at the same time that her mother was an excellent woman. Madame Campan was heard to say, that of all the children entrusted to her care, the best instructed had been brought up by a grandmother.

She did not mean the best instructed in letters, but in piety, in order, in submission, in obedience and in gentleness. We do not maintain that the grandmother should supersede the mother, but only inspire and direct her in those gracious ways which lead to virtue by pleasing example—ways which woman knows, but of which man cannot catch the secret. Such a grand mother it was the privilege of Randolph to have in his home. In addition to her natural gift of high culture, Mrs. Cary possessed rare colloquial powers which made her a charming companion. But above all she was a devout Christian, beautified by the graces of Faith, Hope and Charity. Her charming talent for narrative made her the especial favorite of children, and she was so thoughtful of their pleasures, that she generally had by her a little store of good things for their gratification. There are those whose memory recalls with admiration and gratitude, the form of that venerable woman seated in "the old arm chair" in the sweet parlor at twilight, with the lovely group of grand-children at her knees, looking up into her bright face and drinking in the lessons of wisdom and love which are bearing fruit in eternity, for she has welcomed one of her chief treasures to her Heavenly Home.

If it be true, as a German author has beautifully said, that "every first thing continues forever with a child—that the first color, the first music, the first flower, paint the foreground of life—that every new educator effects less than his predecessor," then

we must conclude that Randolph received in his
own home the seeds that were now beginning to
spring up to view, and soon commenced bearing their
fruits  The Bible which his mother had given him
he diligently read.   Upon entering the High School
he joined the prayer meeting, and his chosen companions were the more pious boys.   In the following summer he expressed a desire to be confirmed,
with some of his schoolfellows in the Seminary
Chapel.   His pastor, Rev. Mr. Johnston, of St.
Paul's Church, Alexandria, naturally wishing to have
the privilege of presenting so gentle a lamb of his
flock for this interesting rite in his own parish
church, Randolph consented to postpone his con-
firmation and made his first profession of religion
by communion in St. Paul's Church, four months
before he reached his fifteenth year.   To show his
conception of the Christian character of which he
had just made profession, we transcribe from his
Diary, commenced about this time, the following
rules of conduct :

"1st. I shall endeavor from this time to adhere to these rules and
at the end of each day review them ; and

2d. Throughout each day I shall try to preserve a sense of the
presence of God, and by this to regulate my actions.

3d. Feeling the salvation of my soul as paramount to all other
aims and that it is my duty to work in Christ's cause in season and
out of season, I will do my best by word and deed to lead others
into the way everlasting.

4th. Never to do anything which I have reason to suppose I may
afterwards repent of, and of which the lawfulness is doubtful.

5th. Not to allow the praises of men to incite me to any wrong action, feeling that I know the sinfulness of my heart better than others;
and to be continually on my guard against pride and the deceits of
the world, the flesh and the devil.

6th. To guard against insincerity and too much levity in conversation.   To endeavor to deny myself in order to be kind and charitable to all around me ; more quick to see the faults of myself than
those of others, knowing that all I have is from God and that all
men are the work of his almighty hand.

7th. To improve every moment of time—to think much of the

shortness of life and that I may at any moment be called away to meet a just God.

8th. Never to do anything out of revenge, or to do anything I should justly think mean in another.

9th. Not to speak evil of another unless some particular good come from it, and not to speak anything that may produce mirthfulness on the Sabbath day.

10th. To inquire every night when I go to bed what good I have done, whether I have been negligent, and what sins I have committed during the day.

11th. To endeavor to grow in the knowledge of myself and of my sins, and continually to compare the great majesty of God with my own littleness, and to trust only in Him to bring me safely through this life."

At the examination at the High School, in June of this year, Randolph took the honors in every class, and came home laden with medals and certificates of proficiency. One of the Examiners expressed his gratification that one of the "old names" was again so distinguished. A newspaper, giving an account of the examination was sent to his friend Mr. Dewy, and elicited a highly complimentary letter, in which he affectionately urged him not to sacrifice his health to his studies.

In the summer of 1859, Randolph took the highest prize at the High School—the "gold medal"—besides many smaller prizes. Mr. McGuire, the Principal of the High School, having been asked by a brother Clergyman who of the boys he had under his charge he considered the most gifted, replied: "Take him altogether, Randolph Fairfax." What were his own private thoughts at this intoxicating period of his life, we learn from his diary, the existence of which was unknown even to his parents until after his death, when two little manuscript books were found among his papers, endorsed "Private." In this record of his daily experience we find the following entries of this date:

"I fear that my worldly occupations are fast drawing my heart from God; that, in my eagerness to be prepared for my school examinations, I forget the great examination which my soul must stand at the bar of God. Oh, that I could despise the things of this world; could lay aside all my vain ambition, and have the glory and service of God as my chief ambition and desire. How little are these vain honors compared with the crown of glory! Oh! that I could estimate them aright, and could see myself as God sees me! Oh, Father have mercy upon me for Christ's sake!"

Again, on Tuesday, 21st of June, we find the following record :

"Oh! that I could always bear in mind that I must one day stand an examination before the Judge of man ; but especially now, while my scholastic examinations are proceeding. I should not allow them to draw my attention from Heaven, but continually remind me of that final judgment. Oh! if I should then be found*wanting ! Oh! Father, grant me Thy grace, keep me from falling, and let not each day pass in forgetfulness of Thee, to whom I owe all my blessings."

## CHAPTER III.

*Randolph at University of Virginia—Professor Minor's Prayer-Meeting—Influence of Professors—Graduation—Rules for spending Sunday.*

From the High School Randolph went to Dinwiddie Academy, in Albemarle. We have but few facts in relation to this year of his life, except the most satisfactory testimonials of his good conduct and proficiency in his studies. He commenced a new diary at this era of his life, in which we find the following record of his estimate of himself, which is in striking contrast to the golden opinions his conduct won from his teachers, school fellows and associates:

"October 19th, 1858.

"Oh, Father, in commencing to record the feelings of my heart, preserve me from all hypocrisy, enable me to deal with my heart in sincerity, and keep me from being deceived in a matter of so much importance as the salvation of my soul. Although I profess to be a servant of God, I feel that my conduct is little different from that of an unconverted soul; that I have not the single eye to God's glory, and that love to Christ, producing love to all mankind, which befit a true Christian. My sinful, deceitful heart is too much engrossed in worldly cares, and the god self is worshipped instead of my Maker. Oh, God, keep me from such vile ingratitude as to spurn the offers of my blessed Saviour, and of rendering Thee the hollow service with which I have formerly been content."

In the fall of 1860 Randolph matriculated at the University of Virginia. His diligence and success in his studies is sufficiently attested by the fact that he graduated with distinction the first session in French, Latin and Mathematics. He does not seem to have been so engrossed by his studies as to have neglected the culture of his soul. He availed himself gladly of the means of grace within his reach.

Among these was a Bible Class, taught by Professor Minor, who, though a Professor of the Law, is not ashamed of the Gospel of Christ, and whose Bible Classes for students in the Chapel of the University, and for servants in his own Parish church, furnish a pleasing example of the manner in which our literary laymen may lay their laurels at the foot of the Cross. It is a matter of devout thankfulness to Almighty God that the influence of the Professors at the University of Virginia has been for so many years so decisively a Christian influence. It is a fact well calculated to arrest the attention of careless young men, and to encourage those who have already commenced a Christian life, to see men eminent in all the walks of science and literature casting the weight of their authority into the scale of Christianity. It is believed that there is not a Professor at the University of Virginia who would not gladly make his attainments tributary to this great end.

From his relative, Julian Fairfax, we have just learned some interesting facts, illustrating Randolph's life at the University. The Christian Association was very flourishing at this time, and Randolph was a very efficient member of it. By this Society the College, including the dormitories proper, and the boarding houses in the neighborhood were laid off in districts. In each of these, prayer-meetings were held every week, and Randolph was a regular and active attendant. By the example of his daily life, no less than by his fervent prayers, he preached the Gospel. Committees were sent out by the Association to hold regular services at destitute places in the vicinity of the University. One of these visited the Poor House, about two and a half miles from college, and read the scriptures to the poor, with brief exhortations and prayers. When Randolph conducted the meeting, he prepared himself by fervent prayer and careful study. His public prayers were earnest and appropriate, and his addresses serious and impressive.

In Nov. 1860, two military companies were formed and tendered their services to the Governor. Randolph was a member of the Southern Guard. These companies, with the volunteer companies of Charlottesville, celebrated Jefferson's birthday by a grand parade. During the parade news came of the attack on Fort Sumter, whereupon a grand salute was fired. Two days afterwards these companies volunteered to accompany the Charlottesville companies to Harper's Ferry. Randolph was very anxious to go, but he was restrained by a letter from home, telling him not to go until he was ordered; and he yielded, as he had ever done, his wishes to the will of his parents.

It was while a student at this institution that he inscribed in his diary the following rules for spending the Sabbath:

"1. Perform my usual devotions and read the chapter for the Bible Class.

2. After Bible Class attend Church, spend the time till dinner in examination, reading and prayer.

3. After dinner read till prayer meeting, and, after prayer meeting, walk with a Christian companion, and endeavor to make the conversation as suitable as possible to Sunday.

4. After supper attend Church, or spend the time in reading, contemplation, &c.

5. Endeavor at all times to remember that it is precious time, and to guard against indolence."

It was during his session at the University of Virginia that the State of Virginia seceded from the United States, and most of the students withdrew and volunteered in the army. Randolph was anxious to follow their example, but, in deference to the wishes and remonstrances of others, he was induced to remain until the end of the session.

## CHAPTER IV.

*Military School at the University— The Battle of Manassas—Randolph enlists in the Rockbridge Artillery—His letters from the Army—His contentment and cheerfulness—Incidents of Camp Life in Fairfax—Review of Stonewall Brigade—Sir James Fergusson— Crossing the Mountains—Gen. Johnson's compliment to the Brigade—Jackson's Farewell, &c.*

During the vacation, the University was converted into a military school, and Randolph passed from the groves of the academy to the *campus martius*. In the meantime the battle of Manassas was fought, and then the University became a hospital. Randolph assisted in receiving and nursing the wounded soldiers, and could no longer resist the call to the field of battle. He repaired to Manassas Junction and enlisted, as a private, on the 12th of August, 1861, in the Rockbridge Battery, then commanded by Captain (now General) Wm. N. Pendleton, and afterwards by Captains (now Majors) McLaughlin and Poague, and more recently by Capt. Graham. For our knowledge of his career as a soldier, we are indebted chiefly to the familiar letters of himself and his mess-mates, from the camp letters, written upon scraps of paper in pencil, and with the off-hand freedom of a family correspondence. Randolph's letters contain a continuous description of Jackson's wonderful campaigns, as they appeared to a boy of 18 years of age in the ranks. This is a point of view from which we do not often look at the evolutions of armies. This fact, by itself, invests these letters with interest. We shall reproduce copious extracts from them because they add something to the materials of history, and are fitted to do good, by their moral and religious tone, their glowing patriotism and the spirit of contentment and cheerfulness which they breathe, in the midst of the severest trials to which a youth so gently nurtured could be exposed. His letters, too, hastily as they have been penned, are characterized by a vein of strong common sense unusual in one so young, and by uncommon sagacity in speculating upon the probable objects of movements in the army, from August 12th to October '61, describe his first impressions of Manassas Junction, which any one who visited it during the winter and fall of '61, would recognize—his walk to Centreville in a drenching rain, over the late battle-field, and his enlistment in the Rockbridge Battery—enumerates his mess-mates, among whom are Kinloch Nelson, Jim Garnett, L. Macon, L. Blackford and "other nice fellows'—his visits to his old friends of the 17th Virginia; his pleasure at hearing the familiar voices of Bishop Johns and the Rev. Mr. Walker, on two successive Sundays; his experience in cooking—his amusement "in seeing ——, with his sleeves rolled up, washing dishes and making up bread"—makes light of the so-called discomforts of camp-life—describes a review of the Virginia troops and presentation of flags by Governor Letcher—a review of the Stonewall Brigade by Generals Johnson, Beauregard and Smith, in the presence of two members of the English Parliament—Sir James Fergusson and the Hon. Mr. Burke—the concentration of troops at Centreville, and the construction of breastworks—the marching and countermarching to Fairfax Court House and Centreville—the picketings at Mason's, Munson's and Upton's hills—rejoices in the open air and active life, and expresses the opinion that with a little precaution, suggested by common sense. a soldier, if he has a good constitution, ought to be more healthy than other men. He represents his

experience of camp as very pleasant so far, and he
has no desire to be an officer. "My situation is
the more desirable of the two—I have none of an
officer's cares and responsibilities—I have as agreeable companions as I have ever had at school or
college—have as many privileges as I desire, and
live as well as most officers, and better than many.
The additional honor is very little in my opinion,
as my experience has shown me that epaulets are
not always criteria of merit. The attraction of
office would not induce me to give up the agreeable
society and companionship, and light duty of my
present situation." He then bewails "the desola-
tion of Fairfax, where barren fields, dilapidated
houses and old camp grounds testify to the rava-
ges of war;" and concludes with the lamentation, "I
am afraid poor old Alexandria will never raise her
head again."

The summer holidays, and drills, and dress pa-
rades were now passed, and he was called to look
at the more serious features of "grim visaged war."
Jackson had been assigned to the command of the
Valley, and had taken leave of his old brigade in
a characteristic speech, concluding with, the now
historical passage, "You were the first brigade in
the Army of the Shenandoah, the first in the Army
of the Potomac, the first in the 2d Corps, and the
first in the affections of your commander." Jackson's command consisted of his old brigade, some
thousands of militia, and Ashby's cavalry. In a
letter dated the 12th of November, Randolph
says:

"Last Friday we marched from 6 A. M. to 7 P. M., stopping only
to water the horses—marching 25 miles, of which I walked 22;
slept that night in a barn—next day crossed the Blue Ridge in a
drenching rain. Many of the men were drinking and disorderly—
reached Berryville that evening, and were quartered in the Court
House. I and three friends were hospitably entertained by Dr.

Kownslar, and actually slept in feather beds without taking cold. We started the next day (Sunday) just as the Church bells were ringing, and marched to Winchester."

November 24th, he writes:

" Our camp is prettily situated among some cedar knolls near Winchester, and is occasionally enlivened by the presence of the ladies."

He speaks of the hospitalities of the Williams' and the Barton's, both of whom had sons in the battery. He says:

" I can hardly realize that this is Sunday, so different from the Sundays of former days. How little did I think, last year, when I was enjoying those delightful Sundays at home, that I should ever spend one in such circumstances. There is, unfortunately, too much truth in the saying, 'there is no Sunday in war.' But Sunday here is perfect enjoyment to what it was at Centreville, where the chief difference between it and other days, seemed to be absence of drills. Yesterday was my 19th birthday, and it makes me quite patriarchal to think of it. I suppose the Lieut. Fairfax, mentioned in the capture of Mason and Slidell, is the person who was our cousin Donald, for I do not care to recognize the relation-ship any longer."

# CHAPTER V.

*The Winter Campaign to Bath and Hancock—His Furlough—
Visit to Richmond and return to Camp at Cedar Creek—The
Battle of Kernstown—Retirement up the Valley—The Battle of
McDowell—Dr. Dabney's Sermon.*

We continue our extracts from Randolph's correspondence, January, 1862:

"Leaving Winchester on the first and marching about 32 miles,
we reached Bath on the 4th, and driving the Yankees out, followed them to the river. That night, and most of the following
day, our Battery was engaged in firing at the town of Hancock,
on the other side of the Potomac, and at the Federal batteries.
I suppose our movement was a feint to cover Gilham's operations
towards Capon Bridge. During this trip my patriotism was put to
a severe test, by marching through the mountains over the icy
roads as smooth as glass—bivouacking at night in the snow, and
rolling the heavy guns up the slippery steeps by day. On the day
we left the Potomac we marched from ten o'clock in the morning
till twelve at night, and only made seven or eight miles. Even
then we did not reach our wagons and had to *sit* around our fires
one of the coldest nights I ever felt. The next day we overtook
our wagons about sundown, and pitched into a good supper which
our cook had prepared for us, having been without food, save a
morsel by the way, for thirty six hours. Three roads meet here
leading to Romney, Winchester and Martinsburg, either of which
we may take.'   •

Jackson took the road to Romney, and in the
meantime Randolph, being determined to re-enlist,
got his first furlough and visited his family in Richmond. When he returned to the field his command
was encamped at Cedar Creek, about two miles
from Strasburg, Jackson having evacuated Winchester and retired from the Valley.

The following is his account of the battle of
Kernstown:                ●

"On the 22d of March, much to our surprise, we took up the
line of march towards Winchester. I suppose the object of the
move was to keep Banks' force in the Valley. We met the ene-

my at Kernstown. The battle began about two o'clock, and raged fiercely until night. Our force was not more than 3,500 infantry, cavalry and artillery, while that of the enemy was more than 10,000. On our way to our position our Battery had to cross a wide open bottom exposed to the fire of the Yankee artillery. Several shells exploded near us, disabling one of our guns. Just before we got into position a shell passed through one of the wheel horses of our third piece and into the other, where it exploded, tearing off the legs of the driver and the foot of a man walking by the gun. It was a horrible sight to see the mangled horses and men lying helpless on the ground. We got into position about three o'clock, and were firing until it was nearly dark. The infantry had by this time fallen back nearly to our position, and our guns were turned to pour canister into the Yankees so soon as they should appear on the edge of the woods. The position was unluckily a bad one, as they were able to come too near under cover of the woods. Consequently our fire was not so effective as it otherwise would have been, although we learned afterwards that it was very destructive. The Yankee Captain, Schriber, says in his report: 'that the Rebels advanced their heavy battery (that was our's) which threw some well directed shots in our (Yankee) battery, and our cavalry and infantry on the slope of the hill, soon rendering it evident that the Rebel battery would have to be taken.'

"This explains the advance of the Yankee infantry on our flank. The Yankee Captain further says, 'that the canister from our battery strewed the ground with dead and dying and broke the infantry that was charging us.'

'Our drivers being raw hands we were so long limbering up that two of our men were wounded, one of our horses struck in three places and his mate in one. In this state we drove off the field while the minnie balls were flying at a most uncomfortable rate, and succeeded in getting our piece into a little hollow in the woods, where our worst wounded horse fell dead. Discovering that we were now between the lines, our Lieutenant ordered us to cut the traces and make the best time in getting away, which we did in Bull Run style. I hated mightily to lose our old piece. It was one taken at Manassas, and one of the best of our six pounders. It is some consolation to think that we got it off the field and only left it when our horse was killed and there was no time to put in another. I have great reason to be thankful to God for my preservation, and that of my friends. My only trust in such times of danger is that I am entirely in God's hands, and He will preserve me until His own good time. Our piece was the last to leave the field.

"I escaped with a bullet hole through the skirt of my coat. Our men acted very gallantly. One of our mess received a letter from his father, Mr. —————— ———— of Winchester, saying that the enemy's loss, as estimated by a person who visited the hospitals, was 800 wounded and 500 killed—while our killed, whom Mr. ———— helped to bury, numbered 85, and our wounded in the ene-

my's hands 92.  Our total loss in killed and wounded was about
425.  I am told that the battle of Kernstown is considered in
Richmond a victory, and I suppose it was, since we inflicted a
heavier loss than we suffered, and gained our object in keeping
their large army occupied by our small one.  Our army has been
increased in numbers since the battle by recruits and drafts from
the militia.  The night after the battle we encamped about four
miles from the field, and leisurely began our retreat the next day
about ten o'clock, eating our dinner at Cedar Creek, and then
marching to our old camp ground, about two miles above Wood-
stock.  The Yankees are at Edinburg on the other side of the
river, and our guns are sent down every few days and have artillery duels with them."

Jackson soon resumed his retreat up the Valley,
and reaching Harrisonburg turned towards the Blue
Ridge, and crossing the Shenandoah took his position in Elk Run valley, near Swift Run Gap.  Here
the troops were exposed for several days to heavy
rains without tents.  On the 16th of May, Randolph
writes from the foot of Shenandoah mountain,
whither Jackson had gone to meet Milroy advancing from towards Monterey:

"Since my last letter, we have been constantly moving.  In
two weeks we have been in the counties of Rockingham, Albemarle, Augusta, Highland and Pendleton, crossing the Blue Ridge
and Shenandoah mountains twice, and have fought a battle on the
western slope of Bull Pasture mountain, at McDowell.  From the
nature of the ground artillery could not be used on our side.  While
the battle was proceeding on the top of the mountain, we were in
camp on this side.  The fight began just before sundown and lasted
until nine o'clock.  Our Brigade marched up the mountain just
before the fight commenced, and was then marched back about
five miles to camp to cook.  It was again sent for, and the firing
ceased just as we reached the top of the mountain the second time.
This movement of Jackson's was a great surprise to the Yankees,
who left behind many tents and stores, and destroyed more.  There
are so many gorges and defiles in these mountains that the pursuit
of the enemy must be slow and cautious or our victory would have
been more fruitful.  I think it probable our next destination will be
Harrisonburg, where, uniting with Ewell, we may, by God's blessing, drive the Yankees out of the Valley.

"I was much pleased with a sermon preached for us last Monday
by Dr. Dabney—the day set apart by Gen. Jackson as a day of rest
and thanksgiving.  The services were held within hearing of the
enemy's guns and were impressive.  Dr. Dabney's view of the war

was that it was a visitation of God upon us for our sins, and that it would not cease until the purpose of God was accomplished—that is, until our people repent and turn to God; or else it may cease for awhile, and when our cup of iniquity is full more terrible punishments may come upon us. He also said, that God sometimes uses a more wicked instrument to punish a more innocent one, but that the punishment of the more wicked instrument would surely fall sooner or later, with terrible vengeance. He spoke of the Babylon of the North and predicted its downfall and destruction. His view is, that nations, as they cannot be punished in the next world are punished in this for national sins—a view I think entirely coinciding with the Bible. I think the fate of the country is now in the hands of the praying people, and though I cannot see how or when, I believe God will certainly answer the prayers of His faithful people in the land. I believe I have not told you of the new discipline of our army. We have come to be veterans—have no tents, carry our knapsack and blankets, never ride on caissons, obey orders implicitly without enquiring the why or wherefore, and, in case of necessity, can live on half rations and not think it anything remarkable. When expecting a fight our rations are six hard crackers and a quarter of a pound of pork a day."

# CHAPTER VI.

*Battles of Front Royal and Winchester—Pursuit of the Yankees to the Potomac—Prisoners and Spoils—Yankee Breastplates—Fremont and Shields.*

Randolph's anticipations were realized. Jackson went in pursuit of the Yankees in the Valley. In his next letter dated the 27th of May, 1862, our young friend says:

"Last Friday we made a forced march from Luray to Front Royal, a distance of twenty-seven miles—surprised the Yankees stationed there, (two regiments with cavalry and artillery) took the town, with a large amount of quartermaster and commissary stores, and about 700 prisoners and two pieces of artillery. And all this with the loss of only two or three killed and wounded. The Yankees left in such a hurry that they did not have time to burn two fine bridges which they had just built across the two branches of the river at that point. By a strange coincidence one of the Yankee regiments was the 1st Maryland, who came into contact with our 1st Maryland, who completely routed the Yankees, chasing them through the town, and taking their camp and colors, and a good many prisoners. Nearly all the remainder of the regiment, with their Colonel, Lieut. Colonel, Major and many captains were brought in that night by the cavalry. The next day we marched on towards Winchester and then struck off to the left to get into the Valley turnpike at Middletown and cut off the Yankee forces at Strasburg. We captured at Strasburg many prisoners and a large amount of medical and other stores, and I have heard a battery of six guns, that was escaping by a by-road to Moorfield.

"This last I am not quite certain about. Our cavalry also captured almost the whole baggage train of the Yankees, consisting of hundreds of wagons. Pushing on all that day and all night without the least rest, driving the Yankees before us, we reached Winchester a little before daybreak. Here the Yankees made a stand and while we attacked them in front, Ewell's division attacked their left flank, on another road. The battle began at early dawn and lasted about two hours and a half, when by a general charge our men drove the Yankees from their position, completely routing them and chasing them at a double quick through Winchester. Such a rout has not been seen since Manassa; arms, knapsacks, blankets and all sorts of accoutrements, were strewn along the route of their flight. We pressed them for five miles beyond Winchester, but the broken down condition of our troops compelled the infantry to stop. The cavalry continued the pursuit. It is impossible for me to form an estimate of our captures. I know that our loss is small, and the number of our prisoners must be near 3,000; the amount of stores, ammunition, &c, is very large. We were exposed to a hot fire from some sharpshooters behind a stone wall, as well as a heavy artillery fire. Poor Bob McKim and another was killed, and we have six men wounded. I can only through the blessings of God that none of us were lost. Our passage through Winchester was perfectly glorious. The pavements were crowded with women, children and old men, waving their handkerchiefs, weeping for joy and shouting as we passed at double-quick. Our troops were loaded with Yankee plunder, and rigged out in Yankee clothes to such an extent, that an order forbidding it was issued, lest it might lead to firing on our own men. Most of our spoils fell to those who happened to be, as this in front had no time to stop. Among other things captured was a wagon load of lemons and one of cake. The lemons were reserved for the sick, but the cakes were disposed of in short order. Among the spoils I have seen two Yankee breast-plates that so much has been said about. They were of different patterns; one a simple steel plate, and the other had points and came down over the hips. Unfortunately for the owners they had no plates behind, where they were most needed. We are now resting. Yesterday was observed as a day of thanksgiving. It is impossible to tell when or where will be our next move."

On the very next day after this letter was written the old brigade, with Carpenter's and McLaughlin's (the Rockbridge) batteries moved towards Charlestown. While our forces were finishing up their work on the Potomac, intelligence was received that Shields was moving from Fredericksburg, and Fremont from the west, with a view of concentrating in Jackson's rear, and cutting him off with his prisoners and spoils. Accordingly our army began to fall back up the Valley on the 30th of May. Ewell had been sent to hold Fremont in check at Strasburg, and the retreat continued to Harrisonburg, with a caravan of prisoners and booty in front, and the eagle-eyed Ashby guarding the rear.

# CHAPTER VII.

*The Battles of Cross Keys and Port Republic—Day of Thanks-giving—Dr. Dabney's Sermon—The Holy Communion.*

The stirring events immediately succeeding, we will allow our young soldier to tell in his own words:

'CAMP NEAR PORT REPUBLIC,  
"June 14th, 1862.

"DEAR MAMA: I have already told you how completely we were surprised last Sunday. We were all lying quietly in camp, expecting to have a day of peace and rest, when we were startled by the sound of cannon in our front. A scene of the utmost confusion ensued. The wagons were packed and our pieces hurried forward as fast as the horses could be hitched. We took position on a commanding hill, opposite Port Republic, from which we could see the Federal columns coming up the road on the other side within easy cannon range. After a brisk cannonade, we drove them back in confusion. Our position was such that they could not bring their cannon to bear upon us, so that all the firing was on our side— a kind of fighting which we all agreed was decidedly the most pleasant we had ever tried. This was the advance of Shields' army, consisting of three or four regiments which had pushed on rapidly. It is said that Gen. Jackson, whose head-quarters were at the Port, was informed of their appearance only a few minutes before they had actually posted their guns around the town, and he narrowly escaped being taken prisoner. The General had just crossed the bridge, when he saw a Yankee gun come down the road on the opposite side and take position so as to command the entrance to the bridge. Taking it for one of our guns, he called out, 'Limber up and come over or the enemy will get you.' The Yankees looked surprised, and then turning their gun upon the General, informed him of their true character by firing a shot at him. One of our pieces happening to arrive at the time, and putting in two well-directed shots, compelled the Yankees to abandon their piece which was afterwards secured by us. Soon after this little affair we heard cannonading to our rear, which was the opening of the battle between Fremont and Ewell's division, our rear guard. The battle raged all day, and we anxiously listened to every shot to tell by the sound which side was gaining ground. The suspense was awful, for we knew that if our forces were driven back our retreating army would be assailed by the force in our rear, and probably be cut to pieces. Towards evening, to our great joy, we could hear the report growing more and more distant, and we soon knew that the enemy had been repulsed. I understand that our centre was posted upon a strong hill which the enemy attacked in front. They led regiment after regiment to the charge and were as often driven back by murderous volleys. Only a part of our force was engaged in this fight ; our brigade and Gen. Taliaferro's were kept to guard the bridge, and some others were held in reserve. That night we were brought over to the east side of the river to camp, fully expecting to return and attack Fremont with our whole force in the morning. But, to our surprise, we were led against the enemy on that side, while the remainder of our forces, who had held their position during the night, were drawn back to our support and the bridge burnt to keep the enemy from following.

Some blame Jackson for not attacking Fremont instead of Shields. But I think he pursued the wiser course. If we had attacked Fremont and been defeated, there was no safe way of retreat, and no General should go into battle without providing a way of retreat in case of defeat. In the Monday's fight with Shields, we had about five or six thousand. The enemy's force was about eight thousand. The battle began soon after daylight, and after a long cannonade, chiefly by the enemy ; during which time our right wing moved around through the woods so as to flank the Yankee position. Our left wing, consisting of our battery and some pieces from other batteries, with several regiments of infantry, advanced to the attack. We were met by almost the whole force of the enemy, and, after a hard struggle, we were compelled to fall back. It seems that our advance was made too soon, so that instead of having our right wing operating in conjunction with us, the enemy were able to meet us with an overpowering force and drive us back before our right was ready to attack. Our battery was posted in an open wheat field, exposed to fire from infantry and artillery. We could see and hear the balls cutting through the wheat on every side, but strange to say, we escaped with but few casualties. Nothing but the mercy of God kept us from suffering severely. As we drove off the field, I thought the day was lost, but soon we heard the firing on our right and our wing returned as soon as the regiments could rally. The complete rout of the enemy soon followed, and five splendid guns and five hundred prisoners were taken. And all this was done in sight of Fremont's army which just then appeared on the heights, on the opposite side of the river, but too late, as there was an unfordable river between us. Our army was drawn back to Brown's Gap, by an old mountain road, the knowledge of which was the key to our whole success. For had we been forced back by the same road we came, we would have been shelled to pieces by the Yankee guns on the opposite side of the river, just as we had shelled them on this day. Our cavalry followed the enemy for ten or twelve miles and came up with the baggage train; all of which would have been captured, some think, if poor lamented Ashby had been there to lead them. I have not been able to ascertain definitely, but I think our loss could not have exceeded 500 wounded, though I see a newspaper exaggerates it to 500 killed and 1,000 wounded. I think that papers that print every idle report they hear are the curse of our country. Fremont has fallen back to New Market and we are resting. Yesterday, June 14th, by special order, services were held in the regiment, giving thanks for our victories and prayers for further blessings. I heard a delightful sermon from Dr. Dabney yesterday evening, and another this morning. This evening the sacrament of the Lord's supper is to be administered and I hope I may be able to attend. It is such a comfort and a great cause for thanksgiving to have such a Christian as Jackson for our General. I have known him when obliged to fight or march on Sunday to set apart another day for rest and divine service. And when other Generals would have continued marching I have known him to lie by and rest on Sunday. No wonder the blessing of God attends his army in such a signal way. I thank God for the glorious success, as He alone can be considered the author of it. I also thank Him sincerely for my preservation during the fight."

# CHAPTER VIII.

*Jackson's on to Richmond—His flank movement on McClellan at the battle of Malvern Hill—Randolph struck by a fragment of shell—His return to Gordonsville—Battle of Cedar Run or Slaughter's Mountain—Retreat—Forward movement—Shelling at Rappahannock—Flank movement on Pope—Battle at Manassas —Advance into Maryland—Capture of Harper's Ferry—Provost Guard at Martinsburg.*

Jackson now flew swooping down from the mountains like an eagle upon McClellan's rear on the Chickahominy, and in cooperation with Lee won the series of brilliant victories around Richmond which have made the names of Coal Harbor, Gaines' Mill, and Malvern Hill historical. The battery to which our young friend belonged was held in reserve until the bloody fight at Malvern Hill. He writes:

"For an hour, we were exposed to the heaviest artillery fire I ever saw. Shot and shell seemed to pour over in one successive stream, and burst in our midst. We lost two killed and ten or twelve wounded in our company. I was struck by a piece of a shell on the collar bone, but fortunately received from it only a bruise which put me on the disabled list yesterday. It was only through God's mercy that our loss was not greater. Numbers were struck by fragments of spent shells which did no serious injury. The poor 17th, of Alexandria, I hear suffered severely. Hector Esches, Charley Whiting and Colonel Marye were taken prisoners. We drove the enemy step by step, capturing many prisoners and much artillery. I pray that God will continue to prosper our armies until our enemies are entirely overthrown. Don't trouble yourself about my promotion. I am content where I am, and perhaps it is best for me to remain where I am. I would not feel right in accepting a position that would take me out of active service. God again in his mercy has preserved me, and none of my friends were severely hurt, for which, and His other mercies, I owe Him a life of gratitude, and pray for grace to lead it."

After three days' leave of absence, which he spent with his family in Richmond, Randolph joined his battery at Gordonsville, and writes on the 7th of August:

"Judging from appearances both sides are gathering their forces for a decisive struggle. I have no doubt of the result if the Yankees will only fight us."

His next letters of the 11th and 13th of August give an account of Jackson's advance into Culpeper, and the battle of Slaughter's Mountain. He says:

"Three pieces of our battery, were under a very hot fire, but it sustained no injury. General Winder, our brigadier, was standing by one of our guns when he was struck. His death is a great loss to us, as he was one of our first officers. Major Andrews, chief of artillery of our division was severely wounded and fell into the enemy's hands. Our brigade fought splendidly, and was complimented by General Jackson who said they had always done well, but this time gloriously. A panic is said to have seized some of the troops which exposed the flank of some regiments and led to disorder and loss. Our victory was complete. The enemy asked for a flag of truce to bury their dead. The force engaged on our side was the 1st, 2d and 3d brigades, one brigade of Ewell's and several of Hill's, which came up during the fight. We were surprised at our fall back to Gordonsville, after our victory. But Jackson has some plan in his head. After again leaving Gordonsville to advance on Pope, we met with no obstacle until we reached the river. The long siege guns of our battery were engaged in an artillery duel with the Yankee batteries on the other side of the river. After several days skirmishing and unintelligible manoeuvres we crossed the river at another ford without any opposition. We then marched day and night, reaching Manassas Junction on the 30th day, taking the Yankees by surprise. It is wonderful how successful Jackson is in his movements. We effected a march along the entire flank of the enemy and reached his rear without his knowledge. Just after reaching Manassas we saw a brigade of Yankees sent from Alexandria to check the supposed cavalry raid, filing down the opposite hills. They advanced in beautiful line of battle up into a semi-circle formed by our infantry and artillery concealed in the valley until our artillery opening upon their flank and rear, they discovered their mistake and retired precipitately. If I may presume to criticise, it seems to me that if we had suffered them to advance further and then closed upon them with our infantry we should have captured the whole lot, but as it was, we took many hundred prisoners. At Manassas Junction a large amount of stores were taken and destroyed. That night we marched by the light of the burning depot and cars in the direction of Sudley church. We had now been marching three days and three nights, with only about four hours sleep during our march. Nothing but exhilaration at our unwonted success kept us up. Here we were at Sudley

Church with about 20,000 men, with Pope in our front, and a large force advancing from Alexandria on our rear. Well might the Yankees think they had us in a trap. But we privates with entire confidence in our generals, were in blissful ignorance of our danger. For two days by maneuvering and fighting we kept them back until about the middle of the second day we saw the long expected Longstreet advancing on our right. At one time we were completely cut off, and four successive couriers from Longstreet to Jackson were captured, but the fifth got through with the glad tidings of his approach, and Jackson is said to have grasped his hand in joy at his coming. The next day (Saturday) about three or four o'clock the enemy attacked us and were driven back at every point. We had a splendid view of the battle from a hill on which our battery was posted. It was the grandest sight that I ever saw. Artillery was blazing from every rise in the valley below, shells bursting in every direction—batteries and horsemen galloping over the field in pursuit; while away off on our right, we could see the long line of Yankee infantry drawn up to oppose Longstreet, and sheets of smoke bursting from their guns. Soon a cloud of smoke enveloped the plain, and we could only hear the successive roar of artillery and rattling of the musketry, gradually becoming more and more distant. I don't think I ever saw such a disproportion in losses—ours being comparatively light, theirs very heavy."

The Rockbridge Battery accompanied Jackson on the march to Maryland from Manassas, and on his return to Martinsburg to clear out the Yankees in our rear, and which resulted in the capture of Harper's Ferry, with valuable stores and munitions, and 11,000 prisoners. The gun to which Randolph belonged with two regiments of infantry was left in Martinsburg as Provost Guard and was sent while there to destroy a bridge near North Mountain Station. Finding the Yankees in too great force for them, they only tore up the railroad track and returned to Martinsburg, In a letter from that place dated September the 14th, he says:

"The prospect of a little rest here is truly delightful. We have now," he adds, "been more than a month without a change of clothes; either marching or fighting nearly every day, and sleeping without shelter. We have been reduced to a degree of raggedness and dirt that is scarcely tolerable, and the worst of it is we had no chance of getting our baggage which was left at the Rappahannock."

In the same letter he speaks of the good conduct of our troops in Maryland—the strictest discipline having been maintained. In reference to the sentiments of the Marylanders he says :

"There are numbers of the people who would receive us gladly and avow their sympathies for the South, were they assured that we would keep possession of the State."

# CHAPTER IX.

*Battle of Sharpsburg—Straggling—Battery transferred to Col. J. T. Brown's Regiment of Reserve Artillery—March to Port Royal—Battle of Fredericksburg—His last letter—His Death—Lt. Col. Lewis Coleman—Lieut. McCorkle—Berkeley Minor—E. Hyde—T. McCorkle.*

On the 3rd of October, 1862, he writes from camp near Bunker Hill:

"The army is now resting and being re-organized. It is unfortunate that we could not have continued active operations, but it is impossible. The men are ragged and barefooted, and the ranks so reduced by straggling that we could only bring half our force into the field. It is shameful. There was not half of our army engaged in the battle of Sharpsburg. The scoundrels were straggling over the country and eating out the hospitable farmers on their way, while their comrades were beating back McClellan. I don't think we could have had more than 40,000 men engaged at Sharpsburg, and yet we repulsed the enemy. But as the more we drove them back the better their position became on the slopes of the mountains, it was clearly our policy to fall back."

On the 20th and 22nd of October, 1862, Randolph says:

"We have been transferred to the Regiment of Col. Thompson Brown, which constitutes the Reserve Artillery of Jackson's Corps. We have thus dissolved partnership with the old First Brigade, and we are all sorry to part with old friends, and dissolve a connection which has existed from the beginning of the war. We have now two splendid twenty pound Parrots. Such heavy guns are generally held in reserve. We think that our General intended the change to relieve us from the active service in which we have always been engaged.

"Gen. Jackson paid us a high compliment at dinner at Mr. Dandridge's, and said we deserved to have rest. The monotony of our present camp life is relieved by drills, guard duty and cooking, and now and then diversified by a corn-detail, when we have to go ten or fifteen miles, and shuck out a wagon load of corn. I happened to be on a corn-detail during the late snow-storm, and we had a terrible time of it working in the cold driving snow without gloves."

After a march of fifteen days, the Rockbridge

# SKETCH OF THE LIFE OF

...ery encamped near Port Royal, on the Rappa-
...nnock river:

"The weather now," (Dec. 7th,) he says, "is intensely cold, and I am afraid many of our poor soldiers are suffering." "Oh, how I wish," he adds, "that this cruel war would cease. I think when peace is declared I shall be like a man just released from prison or a condemned criminal just receiving his pardon. May God bless you and keep you all."

His last letter, which was found in his pocket after his fall, was written to his mother on the 11th of December, the day after the battle of Fredericks-burg opened:

"Remembering your injunction to write immediately after every battle, I hasten to obey it and relieve you of any anxiety on my account that may have been awakened by the engagement of yesterday at Fredericksburg. We were on picket near Port Royal, and although eighteen miles distant, distinctly heard the cannonade; it was the most continuous and rapid I ever heard, lasting from four o'clock till sunset. I think the enemy must have been repulsed once or twice, but at last succeeded in crossing the river, and now have possession of Fredericksburg. They are, however, no better off than they were before. We have heard firing again this morning, up the river, but do not know what it is.

"The day before yesterday we had an affray with the gunboats on the river below. Our battery was sent down, with the long range guns. We only succeeded in getting five or six shots at a boat passing up, but our 26 pounder, with a Whitlock gun, had a sharp duel with five gunboats above. The engagement, I believe, was harmless on both sides."

This was the last letter Randolph Fairfax ever wrote. On the very next day, as the sun went down, amid a storm of roaring guns and shrieking shells, he fell by the side of the gun he had served so well, and

"Death lay upon him like an untimely frost
Upon the fairest flower of all the field."

Berkeley Minor, one of Randolph's most intimate friends, in reference to the battle of Fredericks-burg, says:

"The company never behaved better than on this occasion. I

speak of my own personal knowledge of the second section, that is, the two twenty pound Parrotts, with one of which Randolph and I worked, as the first was placed in a different part of the field by Major Pelham. Lieut. Graham had command of that section, and was highly complimented by Major Pelham. Our section was under the most tremendous fire that any of the company had ever witnessed. We were in position about two hours only, but were under fire long before we got into position. The fire was most terrible about sundown. Then it was that our dear friend fell. We had ceased firing for a while, when Gen. Jackson rode up and ordered all the guns to be shotted and fired simultaneously, and continue firing as fast as possible. This, it appears, drew the fire of almost all the enemy's guns, in range upon us. Such a shower of shot and shell I never saw before and hope never to see again. This lasted until daylight was gone. After dark we brought off our guns."

## E. Hyde, says:

"The piece of shell which was the cause of Randolph's death, entered the corner of the left eye, killing him instantly."

## T. McCorkle, who was at the same gun with Randolph, says:

"That same shell, of which a fragment struck Randolph, badly wounded Lieut. Colonel Coleman and Arthur Robinson, of Baltimore.* Gen. Jackson had left the place where it exploded, a few minutes before. Lieut. McCorkle was near the same gun, but was not killed until shortly afterwards. Thomas McCorkle and Berkeley Minor bore Randolph's body off the field, and that night he and Lieut. McCorkle were buried together by their weeping comrades, not very far from where they fell."

## Lancelot Blackford, who communicates these facts, says:

"Few of the victims of the war have been committed to the earth on the field of glory, with more genuine grief than that which attended the interment of these two young heroes on Saturday night, the 13th of December, 1862."

* " Both of these have since died of their wounds. Coleman was Professor of Latin at the University of Virginia, and Robinson of the best blood of Maryland. Both were Christians and died full of hope."

# CHAPTER X.

*Tributes of his Preceptor—His Comrades—Of his Captain—Of the Commander-in-Chief of the Army of Northern Virginia—Rev. J. P. McGuire—Kinloch Nelson—Lancelot Blackford—H. Graham—Serj't Macon—Berkeley Minor—Jos. Packard—Capt. Poague—General R. E. Lee.*

We have not painted an ideal portrait and written the name of Randolph Fairfax upon it. We have done little more than classify the facts of his short life, and weave them into a continuous narrative. We shall now only add a few testimonials, volunteered by his fellow students and fellow soldiers, who knew him well in times which try men's souls, and where character develops itself as freely as plants in the open air.

Rev. J. P. McGuire, says:

"I am glad to hear that you are preparing a sketch of Randolph Fairfax, persuaded that no worthier subject could occupy your pen.

\*        \*        \*        \*        \*        \*        \*

Confining my reply to the enquiries contained in your letter, let me begin by remarking that a true estimate of him must be formed from the general tenor of his life, rather than from any isolated incident. His character was throughout of the highest order, and perhaps more remarkable for its exquisite finish than for anything else. As a pupil in the High School, as a student, a Christian, there was a uniform consistency—making one day of singular excellence but the representative of all the rest, and giving to the whole a completeness rarely equalled in its strength and loveliness. Intellectually he was undoubtedly one of the first young men of his day. His mind was strong and clear, understanding promptly and thoroughly whatever he studied. A first rate student, he acquired knowledge rapidly and accurately, promising great success and high rank in whatever department of intellectual labor he might select. Morally, I have not known his superior. God endowed him with a strange purity of mind and heart by nature; and then to this added the grace of true religion. With a quick con-

science, and a most sensitive regard to whatever was right,
whatever was proper and becoming ; he was ever ready to resist the slightest offence against a stainless morality. However retiring and unassuming in his general bearing, he was,
nevertheless, constitutionally brave, richly gifted with that
moral courage, the want of which is often the great defect of
men of genius and even of gallant soldiers. Not the slightest
timidity was there; no hesitancy or avoiding of responsibility
where duty was concerned. Brave as Cæsar in the field of battle, he was not less so for truth and right in public and private,
in the most retired walks of life or amidst a crowd of gay and
thoughtless school boys, or the tempting fascinations of the
social circle. Nothing could exceed the modesty which threw
such a charm around him ; nothing that native politeness,
that unselfish courtesy, which attracted to him so many de-
voted hearts, unless, indeed, it was this steadiness, this quiet
firmness with which he declined evil associations. and preserved the purity with which his divine Lord had blessed him.
To this Heavenly grace it, of course, must be ascribed that
he stood so " clearly in the light of God," and reflected so
much of the Saviour's image. The uncommon purity and
blamelessness of his whole life cannot be accounted for without looking to those spiritual influences which alone sanctify
the heart, and clothe life in the beauty of holiness. Early he
had, no doubt, received them from the God and Father of all,
whose blessed spirit quickens in life's early dawn more of the
children of men than we are apt to think.

  *  *  *  Without intending to compare him with
others, particularly among his fellow-students, for so many of
whom I have the highest admiration, and, hoping that I may
not be deemed extravagant, yet I may not hesitate to say, in
conclusion, that no nobler son was ever born within this grand
old Commonwealth than Randolph Fairfax.

## Kinloch Nelson, now a Lieutenant of Ordnance in Kemper's Brigade, says :

"My acquaintance with Randolph Fairfax commenced at the
High School, in the fall of 1857, where his modest manners, and
unselfish disposition, endeared him to all around him. There an
intimacy began between us, which the lapse of time only strength-
ened, and which was broken by the rude hand of death alone. In
the next summer he became a member of the Episcopal church,
and during the following five years I can truly say, that I never
saw him guilty of a single act inconsistent with his profession. At
the University, we were constantly together, and in the army we

were intimately associated as messmates, and he continued a faithful soldier, alike of his country and of his God. He was among the first to re-enlist in the spring of 1862, and he never lost a day from sickness or absence without leave. At Malvern Hill, he was struck on the chest by a fragment of a shell, and turned to leave the field, but when after walking a few steps, he found it was but a slight wound, he returned to his post, and remained until the battery was ordered to leave the field. In the patient endurance of all the hardships of a soldier's life few equalled him—in unfaltering courage, in that most trying arena, the battle field, none surpassed him. Throughout that whole campaign which shed such an undying lustre on the name of Jackson— from the Romney expedition to the fatal field of Fredericksburg—none ever heard him murmur, none ever saw him flinch? In all those trying marches, he was uncomplaining; alike under the frosts of winter and the burning suns of summer; on all those bloody fields he was ever the model of a christian soldier. I know that none attain perfection in this life, but I should inscribe upon his tomb "Mark the perfect man and behold the upright, for the end of that man is peace.'"

Sergeant L. S. Macon, of the Rockbridge Battery, now the Sheriff of Albemarle, who was one of Randolph's messmates, says:

" He was ever the noble self-sacrificing boy who commanded the admiration of all around him. As a soldier he was surpassed by none. He never swerved from the path of duty, and he met danger even at the cannon's mouth, with unfaltering courage. As a christian, he was sincere and consistent; conscientious in the discharge of the duties of every post; and from his daily life, there was reflected a light which always makes an unmistakable impress, but especially in the bloody strife of the battle field, and in the daily intercourse of camp life. In many situations I have seen him severely tested, and in all he evinced the same heroism. In cold, hunger, or fatigue, I never heard him murmur. He was ever ready to share his comfort, and partake of other's hardships. Truly it may be said of him

He lives upon all memories,
Though with the buried gone."

Lancelot Blackford, also one of his messmates, in delineating his character, says:

" That one of his most striking traits was his modesty. Of all the people I have ever known, he did and said the least to advance his own credit, and to draw attention to anything praiseworthy of himself. A fit accompaniment to his modesty, was his singular purity. In this respect he was in camp what he was in the company of his mother and sisters. Certainly I never saw the man who was more free from the defilements contracted in the midst of this naughty world. The purity of his speech and conduct, which exerted such influence upon his companions, sprang from the purity of his heart; which in him was the fruit of habitual abiding with him of the Holy Spirit. Ran. was always attentive to religious duties; he had a well worn pocket testament, which was each day the man of his counsel. I well remember how under the most adverse circumstances, he always found time to read it; and the solemn earnest expression of his countenance when pouring over the sacred pages. He lost his prayer book in the Potomac the night he dropped his overcoat, blankets, &c. It was but seldom that we were able to spend Sunday appropriately. Sometimes, however, we were quiet enough, particularly between the battles of Richmond and Cedar Run. On these occasions, we spent Sunday as far as practicable together, except when Divine service was accessible, or we had prayer meetings. In our knapsack tent, we frequently read together the whole or parts of the church service, including many of the occasional prayers and thanksgivings. We were both much attached to the Liturgy, and took much pleasure in the use of its forms when unable to attend the public services of the church. The hardships of the Bath and Romney expedition were great, and the complaints of the men not unfrequent; but he never complained. Such was his character, whether undergoing hardships, or enduring the scarcely less painful trial of performing the menial duties which fall to the lot of every private soldier, particularly in artillery service. I have seen him when detailed as teamster from the 15th of July to the last of August, after a fatiguing day's march, and just as we were about to retire to rest, called up to go in the dark for forage to feed his teams. Yet he bore all these exacting duties, such as watering, feeding, currying, and harnessing horses, with such equanimity and sweetness as to strike all his associates. The refined gentleman made a first rate ostler when the exigency demanded it, because he considered it incumbent on him to do his duty in everything that became a soldier. We had few men who were regarded as he was by our captain and other officers. This was the subject of almost the last conversation I had with one of them, 1st Lieutenant Graham. The point upon which all officers and men chiefly agreed in admiring him, was his unswerving devotion to duty, whether in camp or in action. Members of the company in lamenting his fall, would remark with emphasis 'what a good soldier Fairfax was.'"

## Berkeley Minor, says :

"I knew Randolph Fairfax at the University quite well, but not so intimately as I did after he joined this company, (the Rockbridge Battery.) For several months before his death, I was his messmate and bed-fellow, and was able to note more fully the tone of earnest piety that pervaded his words and actions. He was unselfish, modest, and uniformly kind and considerate to all. If there was one trait in him more striking than others, it was his calm, earnest, trustful demeanor in time of battle, resulting I believe from his abiding trust in the Providence and love of God. Many fine young men have been removed by death from the company, yet I do not think that any has been more deeply and universally lamented than he."

Joseph Packard, another of his comrades, says:

"His cheerful courage, his coolness and steadiness, made him conspicuous in every battle field. At the battle of Malvern Hill where he had received a wound, which nine out of ten would have considered an excuse for retiring from the awful scene, he persisted in remaining at his post; and did the work of two, until the battery left the field. But it was in the bearing more than in the daring of the soldier's life that his lovely character displayed itself. He never avoided the most irksome and trying duties. If he had selfishness, those who knew him long and well, as schoolmate and comrade never discerned it. More than once I have heard his beautiful Christian example spoken of by irreligious comrades. When I heard of his death, though only the bare fact was stated, I knew that he had died at his post, in the path of duty and heroic self-sacrifice. Bitter and inexplicable as may be the Providence which has removed one so full of promise of good to his fellows, I feel that we may thank God, that we have been permitted to witness a life so Christ like, terminated by a death so noble."

Captain Poague, commanding the Rockbridge Battery, says in a letter to his father:

"In simple justice to your son I desire to express my high appreciation of his noble character as a soldier, a christian and a gentleman. Modest and courteous in his deportment, charitable and unselfish in his disposition, cheerful and conscientious in his performance of duty, and upright and consistent in his walk and conversation, he was a universal favorite in the company, and greatly beloved by his friends. I don't think I have ever known a young man whose life was so free from the frailties of human nature, and whose character in all its aspects formed so faultless a model for the imitation of others. Had his influence been restricted to the silent power and beauty of his example, his life on earth, short as it was, would not have been in vain. The name of Randolph Fairfax will not soon be forgotten by his comrades, and his family may be assured that there are many who, strangers as they are, deeply sympathise with them in their bereavement."

The following from Gen. Lee will be a fit climax to the foregoing tributes:

CAMP FREDERICKSBURG, Dec. 28th, 1862.

My Dear Doctor :—

I have grieved most deeply at the death of your noble son. I have watched his conduct from the commencement of the war, and have pointed with pride to the patriotism, self-denial and manliness of character he has exhibited. I had hoped that an opportunity would have occurred for the promotion he deserved ; not that it would have elevated him, but have shown that his devotion to duty was appreciated by his country. Such an opportunity would undoubtedly have occurred ; but he has been translated to a better world, for which his purity and his piety have eminently fitted him. You do not require to be told how great his gain. It is the living for whom I sorrow. I beg you will offer to Mrs. Fairfax and your daughters, my heartfelt sympathy, for I know the depth of their grief. That God may give you and them strength to bear this great affliction is the earnest prayer of your early friend,

R. E. LEE.

DR. ORLANDO FAIRFAX.

An enthusiastic soldier after reading Gen. Lee's letter exclaimed : "Such an honor were indeed worth dying for." Another soldier not less enthusiastic said : "The original of this letter if addressed to me under similar circumstances, I should preserve as the most precious I ever received—a thing to be handed down to the latest posterity—a testimonial which a stranger would regard centuries hence as in itself a Patent of Nobility."

# CHAPTER XI.

*Analysis of his Character, its Symmetry, its Root—The Man of the World and the Christian—Faith and Sense—His Standard—Extract from one of his Essays—The Ground of his Hope—His Diary.*

Lord Bacon says a man that is young in years, may be old in hours. The subject of this sketch lived just twenty years and twenty days. If we measure his life by years, it was short, and we may say of him that he came up and was cut down like a flower. If we measure it by the number of events, it was long, for it was crowded with events. To have been in one great battle for his country is an era in a man's life never forgotten, and to which he always refers with pride. Randolph Fairfax in the space of sixteen months, was in ten fierce battles and many intervening skirmishes. To have received the approbation of his teacher, taken the honors of his school, and won the hearts of his fellow students are not common events. To have attracted the attention and elicited the commendation of his commanders, is an honor to the soldier in the ranks. But to have won the unanimous applause of his comrades, not merely for courage in action, patience in suffering and for uniform devotion to duty, but to have gained their esteem and affection, by all those nameless graces which beautified his daily life in camp, is a higher honor still. If we analyse his life and character, to detect the secret of his popularity and success, we shall not find it in the prominence of any one or two traits. Some men had as much genius—others as high culture—some as fine a person—others as much modesty, piety, sweetness of temper and gentleness of man-

ners. It was, that these elements were so mixed
in him, as to make his character round and sym-
metrical.* If we search for the germ of such a
character we shall find it to be a deeply rooted religious principle, of which his life was the normal
development. He seemed to have, we learn from
his diary, an habitual sense of the presence of God—
hearing his word, witnessing his actions and looking at his heart. He lived as in the great task-
master's eye. This is the essential difference between a Christian and a man of the world. The
worldly man only looks at things tangible, visible
and temporal. He has no perception of spiritual
things. He sees only by the light of his natural facul-
ties. Faith is the evidence of things not seen—it
passes the bounds of sense and imparts to invisible
and eternal things the life and power of waking
certainties and actual existences. This is the victory that overcometh the world, even our faith.

Again, our young friend, as we see by an inspec-
tion of his diary, did not measure himself by any
human standard. He daily looked unto Jesus.
His model was "God manifest in the flesh." He
aspired after conformity to His image, who did no
sin and yet died for the sins of others. As Randolph himself says, in a manuscript essay which
now lies before us:

"Where can we find such an example of courage in doing
duty as in the life of the 'man of sorrows' who endured the
cross, despising the shame? Truly this is an example to follow, though we may never attain, till, perfected by him, we
sit down in His kingdom."

* *Totus Teresque Rotundus.*

## CHAPTER XII.

*No incompatibility between the Life of the Soldier and that of the Christian—Courage and Christianity compatible—The highest type of bravery is the man who fears God and who has no other fear.*

Randolph Fairfax adds another to the many pleasing illustrations furnished by this war, of the truth, that there is nothing incompatible between the life of a Christian and that of a soldier. Indeed, other things being equal, a conscientious Christian should make the best soldier. He will not straggle from the ranks, skulk his duty nor desert his colors. Although war is in general inconsistent with the genius of Christianity, and wars of ambition or covetousness, for conquest or subjugation, are specially wicked as to those who are responsible for them; yet, even in such cases, it may be incumbent on a christian citizen to take up arms in obedience to the powers "that be." When soldiers asked John the Baptist what they must do, he did not raise a question as to the lawfulness of war in general, or of the particular wars in which they were enlisted, but dismissed them with the comprehensive precept—Do violence to no man, and be content with your wages—that is— do your duty without murmuring and without any wanton violation of the rights of others. As to defensive wars, it seems to be generally agreed that they are lawful. The same instinct that prompts an innocent bird to defend its nest and its helpless young, justifies man in defending his home, his wife and his children—his rights of person and of property against lawless aggression. And the soldier who fights and falls in such a cause, not only obeys instincts which are a law of nature, but is a martyr to principle.

Such examples also prove that Christianity and courage are not incompatible. There is a vulgar notion that a Christian must needs be a coward. This notion is founded upon the error that he only is the brave man who resents every insult with blows or with arms. According to this notion, a game-cock is the bravest of animals and a vulgar bully the bravest of men. But the truth is, that fighting of itself is no proof of courage at all. On the contrary, it is often the result of cowardice, having no higher motive than the jeers and scoffs of other men. This deference to opinion is one of the most powerful motives of human conduct, and sometimes screws the courage of the most abject cowards up to the fighting point. Many cowards would face the pistol or the cannon, and quail before the finger of scorn pointed by men whom they despise. If we were called upon to define a brave man, we should say of him that he was a man who fears God and who has no other fear. That such were the principles of Randolph Fairfax, we learn from an essay on moral courage, written by him before the war, in which he contrasts the death of a soldier, sacrificing his life on the field of battle from a mere sense of honor, with the death of a Christian martyr, dying from a sense of duty :

"The soldier," he says, "encouraged by the shouts of his comrades and the stirring blasts of the bugle, and knowing that a more certain death and disgrace awaits him should he yield to the base impulses of his nature, may perform prodigies of valor, and, rushing through storms of shot, meet death at the cannon's mouth. Contrast him with the martyr who, rather than abjure his faith and depart from the path of duty, endures the scoffs of a misguided rabble and dies a death many times more terrible than that of the soldier. How vastly superior is the courage of the man who surmounts all difficulties and braves all dangers from a sense of duty."

These principles our young friend not merely

maintained in theory, but he illustrated them in his life and sealed them with his blood.

> He only lived but till he was a man,
> The which no sooner had his prowess confirmed,
> In the unshrinking station where he fought;
> But like a man he died.

One might well suppose that a young man so much admired, beloved and lauded as we have seen that Randolph Fairfax was, by his fellow-students and fellow-soldiers, would be likely to have more of the spirit of the Pharisee than of the Publican. But it would seem that the higher a man rises above the earth, and the nearer his vision of God, the deeper is his insight into his own heart. When we only hear of God by the hearing of the ear, we may have a good opinion of ourselves, but when we see him with the eye of faith we *abhor ourselves*, and repent in dust and ashes. That this was the case with our young friend, will appear in the daily record of his experience made when he was alone with God, and which he never dreamed would be seen by the eye of man; for no one knew of its existence until after his death. We make a few more extracts from it, which are a fair sample of the whole book:

"How little do 1 know of myself, oh God! I know that my heart is deceitful above all things, and I pray Thee to make it known to me, that I may cast all the burden of my sin upon Christ, and obtain a new heart. Oh, Father, reveal thyself to me, through thy Son, and shed abroad thy love in my heart. Let me not deceive myself by any appearance of holiness, but may I forget those things which are behind, and press forward towards Thee. Oh when shall I cease sinning and be truly regenerated by the Holy Spirit? My heart is not influenced as it ought to be by the love of God, or how could I find it so hard to serve him? Oh God put thy fear in my heart, and let not the fear of man keep me from my duty. Oh reveal thyself to me and show me my deep sinfulness, and show me, also, my Saviour on the cross, and enable me to go to him. Wean me from this sinful world; soften my heart,

and give me a single eye to **thy** glory. Grant me **grace to**
keep all my good resolutions, not trusting in my own **strength,**
which is weakness, but in thine almighty aid, **which can**
make me truly one of thy servants, although I **am so sinful.**"

Again :

" Another Sabbath is past, and how **have I** improved my
opportunities? Have I grown in **grace?** My soul sinks
within me when I reflect upon these questions. I have sinned
against the great majesty of God in not worshipping him with
my whole heart. I have partaken of the Holy Communion,
and I hope to the good of my soul ; but if not, how great is
my danger? Do I love God, or no, is a question which tries
my very heart. Oh God, if I have never loved thee before,
help me to begin to-day. Oh, how hard my heart seems. I
can think of God, but he seems like some great being afar
off, whom I can never reach. My faith is so small. Oh reveal thyself to me ; my heart is so proud and sinful, and so
much actuated by the praises of men. Oh God, humble me
in the dust—teach me to know myself, and make thyself
known to me through my crucified Lord. Make the union
between thy spirit and mine closer and **closer.**"

Such was Randolph Fairfax's estimate of himself
when alone with God, whose all-seeing eye was
shining through him, revealing every mote to his
own eye. While the mouths of others were ringing with his praises, he laid his hand upon his own
mouth in the dark, and cried, " God be merciful to
me, a sinner." Such is the history of a private in
the ranks, which we dedicate to the privates of the
Confederate army. May they follow the example
of his life as he followed Christ, and may his death
inspire them with renewed devotion to the cause
which drew from his bleeding heart its last libation.

How glorious fall the valiant, sword in hand,
In front of battle for their native land ;
But, oh, what ills await the wretch that yields—
A recreant outcast from his country's fields.
The mother whom he loves shall quit her home,
An aged father at his side shall roam ;
His little ones shall weeping with him go,
And a young wife participate his woe ;
While scorned and scowled upon by every face,
They pine for food, and beg from place to place.

48 SKETCH OF THE LIFE OF

Stain of his breed—dishonoring manhood's form.—
All ills shall cleave to him. Affliction's storm
Shall blind him, wandering in the vale of tears,
'Till lost to all but ignominious fears ;
He shall not blush to leave a recreant's name,
And children, like himself, enured to shame.

But we will combat for our fathers' land,
And we will drain the life blood where we stand,
To save our children. Fight ye side by side,
And serried close ye men of youthful pride,
Disdaining fear, and deeming light the cost,
Or life itself in glorious battle lost.

Leave not our sires to stem the unequal fight,
Whose limbs are nerved no more with buoyant might
Nor lagging backward, let the younger breast,
Permit the man of age, (a sight unblessed,)
To welter in the combat's foremost thrust,
His hoary head disheveled in the dust,
And venerable bosom, bleeding, burst.

But youth's fair form, though fallen, is ever fair,
And beautiful in death the boy appears;
The hero boy, that dies in blooming years ;
In man's regret he lives, and woman's tears.
More sacred than in life, and lovelier far
For having perished in the front of war.

www.ingramcontent.com/pod-product-compliance
Lightning Source LLC
Chambersburg PA
CBHW022042080426
42733CB00007B/946